*Dizzy*

# Dizzy

## John Birks Gillespie in His 75th Year

**COMPILED AND EDITED** *by Lee Tanner*

**WITH AN INTRODUCTION** *by Jeff Kaliss*   **AND AN ESSAY** *by Gene Lees*

POMEGRANATE ARTBOOKS  •  SAN FRANCISCO

*Photographers*

William Claxton

Michael Collopy

Andy Freeberg

Carol Friedman

Dany Gignoux

William P. Gottlieb

Tad Hershorn

W. Patrick Hinely

Milton J. Hinton

Herman Leonard

Jim Marshall

Giuseppe Pino

Bruce Polonsky

Jeff Sedlik

Herb Snitzer

Charles Stewart

Jerry Stoll

Lee Tanner

Marlene Wallace

Michael Wilderman

*For John Birks Gillespie, of course.*

*And for Fred Robbins and Symphony Sid Torin, two master communicators, who introduced Dizzy—and Bird, Monk, et al—to a vast NYC radio audience, and made damned sure we got their message.*

*And for Linda, my inspiration.*

High-contrast photos of Dizzy on pages 1 and 35: Newport Jazz Festival, Newport, Rhode Island, 1963, © Lee Tanner.

"Waiting for Dizzy," by Gene Lees: Copyright © 1991 by Gene Lees. Reprinted by permission of Oxford University Press, Inc.     Introduction © Jeff Kaliss.

Published by Pomegranate Artbooks. Box 808022. Petaluma, California 94975. © Pomegranate Artbooks.     ISBN 1-56640-396-0. LC 92-61902     Printed in Hong Kong. First Edition

# Acknowledgments

I greatly appreciate the superb contributions of all the photographers. Special thanks to Gene Lees and Jeff Kaliss for their writings, to Lee Hildebrand for his diligent search through jazz literature to find the many comments by and about Dizzy, and to John Turner for his expert help with all matters photographic. Thanks also to Oxford University Press for giving permission to reprint Gene Lees's essay "Waiting for Dizzy."

This project was very much a labor of love and its success was facilitated by the encouragement and support of two couples who share a common devotion to the arts, Kimball and Jane Allen and Tom and Katie Burke. Thanks!

Lee Tanner

In May 1985, not long after Zoot Sims died, Jane and Kimball Allen and Sharlene Hirsch produced a benefit concert at Kimball's in San Francisco with the proceeds going to a scholarship fund for needy high school saxophonists. It was a glorious evening with so many of Zoot's buddies like Al Cohn, Dave Frischberg, Pete and Conte Condoli, Jimmy Rowles, Stan Getz and Herbie Steward playing in heartfelt tribute. Having been particularly friendly with Zoot over the years, it dawned on me that a visual tribute would be in order as well; and rather than show just my own work, I decided to gather a collection from a number of photographers including Bill Claxton, Milt Hinton, David Gahr, Tom Copi, Herb Snitzer and others. Following the one-night exhibition, the collection was presented to Zoot's widow, Louise.

This event was the nucleus of the idea to produce group exhibitions of jazz photography on a regular basis, and the wish became a reality in 1990 when I opened the first of *The Jazz Image* exhibits at Kimball's East across the Bay Bridge in Emeryville. The new jazz club and restaurant is an elegant venue seating up to 400 patrons, and the Allens included gallery space with just such exhibitions in mind. *The Jazz Image* has since become a regular and very popular series. When Dizzy Gillespie was booked for February 1992 following his triumphant month at New York City's Blue Note that kicked off this 75th birthday year, it was agreed to continue the celebration with a special edition of *The Jazz Image* entitled "The Many Views of John Birks Gillespie." The collection of about fifty photographs by some of the most renowned jazz photographers goes back to Gillespie's early days with Cab Calloway, on 52nd Street, at the Royal Roost and at Birdland (some of which I experienced firsthand, though I did not start to photograph until the early 1950s) through to the present at Kimball's East. This show has delighted viewers for five months and is slated to travel to other locations in conjunction with upcoming Dizzy Gillespie celebrations. The following pages preserve this event and give tribute to one of the most remarkable and innovative musicians of our times.

From all of us who have reveled in your creativity and enjoyed your company, thank you John Birks Gillespie!

Lee Tanner
Berkeley, August 1992

During the last few years of digging Dizzy in the flesh, I realized that John Birks Gillespie is like a one-man walking jazz festival. Body and soul, he spans not only the global and historical breadth of the music but also its bubbling, uncontainable spirit.

Legend has it that after wandering north from his South Carolina birthplace in the 1930s, Dizzy drew his nickname because he carried his horn around in a paper bag. But it was the other kinds of bags he kept it in, brand new ones, which began to separate the more innovative of his fellow musicians from the conservative and suspicious majority. His Vandyke beard and clashing wardrobe helped ensure his alienation from the squares.

But he always had his champions. In New York, the then skinny Dizzy rubbed raised elbows with his own chosen Gabriel, in the person of Roy Eldridge, as well as with such hornsmen of his own age as Cuban-born Mario Bauza, who had secured an enviable gig with the Cab Calloway Orchestra.

Bauza, now an octogenarian, laughs while telling me about Dizzy's struggle to make his boundless imagination fit into the scene. "He said to me, 'How you get into big band jobs and I can't?' And I said, 'Because your biggest enemy is the musicians. They don't want you nowhere near them. You got something so progressive!'"

Subsequently, the Cuban decided to pretend to be sick and to send Dizzy as a last-minute replacement. "I stayed 'sick' three days," Bauza recounts. "And the fourth day I came back to my job, and Cab say to me, 'How you like that new fella?' And I say, 'He ain't bad.' Two days later Cab say, 'Do you want that guy in the band?' I say, 'We need this guy. Once you really hear what this guy has to offer, you progress the band.'"

Soon both Bauza and Gillespie outgrew Calloway. Bauza left to help organize the Machito Band, and Dizzy began brewing what would be bebop with a small combo on 52nd Street. The two friends met up again when Dizzy was offered a concert gig and had the foresight, which he's kept clear through his life, to look beyond other people's boundaries.

"I don't remember if it was Carnegie Hall or Town Hall," says Bauza, "but he said, 'I don't know what to do.' I said, 'What do you mean? Why don't you play my music?' He said, 'I don't know nothing about the rhythm.' I said, 'I got a man who got in from Cuba a few months ago, name Chano Pozo, and I'm gonna take you to meet this guy.' I took him to Harlem, to 111th Street. Chano couldn't talk English yet. I said, 'Chano, take that conga and hum some of the stuff you got for this man.' So he hummed that 'Manteca' thing, and when Dizzy heard that, he flipped.

They got together, played that concert, and boom-boom-boom. And that was the beginning."

Through the 1940s, Dizzy presided over the double infusion of Latin and bebop into jazz, sometimes combined under the rubric of Cubop. While he toured his own big band, his search for a wider soul kept him awake in the after-hours clubs of Harlem and San Francisco's Fillmore District, sometimes in the company of his "magic man," Charlies "Bird" Parker. Reminiscing about those heady endless nights, Dizzy told me, "Those were the glory years, when the bubble burst into a new age."

Dizzy kept busy through the decades, recording over 500 albums and making many times that number of friends in many countries. His high-register, staccato instrumental style made him particularly popular in Africa and Latin America. "Latin guys play better jazz than jazz musicians play Latin," Dizzy confided to me. "The music of Cuba, Brazil, the West Indies and the United States is like a flower, with many, many different colors." Although I know that he has adopted the Baha'i faith, I cannot help but envision him as a smiling goodwill Buddha, gently holding that flower.

In 1985 Dizzy was given a big bear hug by Fidel Castro, welcoming him to Cuba. A few years later, he was proclaimed an African chief in Nigeria and was given the honorary title of King of Entertainers. With more such ambassadors, the world might turn more harmonious. "I feel that Dizzy always used his knowledge as a streetwise guy to be around the world musically," comments Brazil-born percussionist Airto Moreira, who toured with Dizzy and vocalist Flora Purim, Moreira's wife, in the United States and Europe. "All you have to give him are the basics, and he can translate it immediately."

These days, Dizzy is still a walking festival. Blissed out at the thirty-third annual jazzfest at Monterey in 1989, he was sur-

rounded by smiling fans and fellow players everywhere as he moved around the fairgrounds. Away from the throng, he presided over a starry-eyed high school all-star band, rehearsing his classic adaptation of the Cuban *Manteca*. The kids soaked up every detail of their hero's meticulous instruction. Later, he advised an attentive press corps that "in another fifteen years, the music of the Western Hemisphere will be unified. And it will be a bigger music, like a musical bouillabaisse."

A few months later, Dizzy dropped in unexpectedly on an early crowd in the lobby/gallery of the elegant Kimball's East jazz club in Emeryville, California, celebrating the opening of *The Jazz Image III*, third of a series of exhibitions of legendary photographs of jazz giants, curated by veteran lensman Lee Tanner, the man behind this book. As Dizzy wandered unassumingly, gazing at the portraits of friends living and gone, he once again inspired a feeling of festival with his intoxicating mixture of humor and reverence.

You will get the same hit off the images of five decades of Dizzy himself, gathered by Tanner for the special exhibit and now found between the covers of this volume. The work of a talented and varied team of photographers, they testify to the man's place in both the evolution of jazz from big band to bebop and beyond, and in the hearts of the women and men who helped him do it.

Among Dizzy's many contributions to the standard jazz book, probably the best-known composition is a testament to global consciousness, both in its rhythms, its exotic melody and its title. Still in demand, the song has been getting the same introduction by its creator for years, and it still scores. "It has withstood the vicissitudes of the contingent world and moved in an odyssey to the rim of the metaphysical," he announces from the stage, adding after a pause, "No shit." The description applies as aptly to Dizzy as to 'A Night In . . . ,' "Whatever name you want on the end."

The details of Dizzy's career contributions are more entertainingly reflected in this collection of pictures than in any thousands of words. But you will get a kick out of Gene Lees's graceful time-traveling reminiscence, "Waiting for Dizzy," just before the photographs start. Those who make music for a living, such as reedman Mel Martin (who featured Dizzy and his rarer compositions on a recent recording by the band Bebop and Beyond) are quick to remind us that the man serves us even better as a living flesh-and-blood resource than as a legend. "He's hitting high G's, playing fantastically lyrical, beautiful solos," reports Martin. "Playing next to Dizzy, I found out that this man digs so deep inside himself for this music, and that's what it's about. That's what Charlie Parker, Thelonious Monk and Bud Powell did, too."

Dizzy sometimes misses the acoustic glory days and the departed pioneers. "I'd be lying if I said I didn't," he admitted during a late-night reverie. "With guys like Coleman Hawkins, Lester Young, Chu Berry, Ben Webster, Roy Eldridge and Red Allen . . . a whole lotta guys dead. I don't *know* many people alive."

Actually, he has made it a point to get to know and perform with a lot of young players, helping them to develop and survive in the less-than-benign environment of the contemporary music business. "First, stay away from dope," he tells them. "And stay away from cigarettes," he adds, with an off-hand puff on a cigar. "Get the proper education, and be prepared for anything that comes along."

What is coming along in these pages is a sort of illustrated education about what love and jazz look like, wrapped up in one cherub-cheeked trumpet player. That is a vital and unending lesson for all of us.

It felt strange, going out there. And we got lost. "This isn't it," Benny Golson said, as the driver of the van pulled into the parking lot by an office building in Englewood Cliffs, New Jersey. Art Farmer concurred. It looked unfamiliar to me, but then I hadn't been to Rudy van Gelder's recording studio in twenty-five years and was disoriented by the new buildings along what once was a country highway. I had last come out here for the *Bill Evans with Symphony Orchestra* session that Creed Taylor produced for Verve. That was in 1965.

We left the parking lot and traveled a little farther. Benny said, "I think this is it," and the driver pulled into a lane among trees, running in an S-shape in a mini-woodland and strewn with puddles from last night's rain, and suddenly there was the cement block building with a high-peaked roof that Rudy van Gelder had built a good thirty years ago to capture some of the acoustic qualities of a church. A sign affixed by the door advised all ye who entered here that there was to be no smoking or drinking within these walls. Rudy said cigarette smoke penetrated and damaged recording equipment. Everyone who had ever recorded here knew Rudy's quirks, and one of them was that you never touched his equipment.

"You know," Art Farmer said, in his low slow voice and with a somewhat grave and almost frowning expression he takes on when he is about to lay something funny on you, "Jim Hall and Red Mitchell have the classic story about Rudy. Red went to high school with Rudy. Red and Jim were here doing a duo record. They talked about the sound they wanted, and Red was in the control room with Rudy, and Red said, 'You know, Rudy, maybe if we just put a little more of this in there.' And he touched one of those faders, and Rudy said, 'That's it. You don't owe me anything. Just pack up and get out.'"

Benny laughed. "He pushed friendship a little too far."

"That was it," Art said. "If you touched anything in his control room . . ."

We went into the building. The studio was immediately familiar: the peaked wooden ceiling, the cement block walls, the recording booth. Rudy still wore cotton gloves when he left the booth to adjust a microphone in the studio. I asked him why he did it. He said, "I'll tell you why I do it. Because it doesn't leave fingerprints on the microphones."

Rudy looked much the same. So did Creed Taylor, youthful—almost boyish—at sixty. A Southerner with family roots in New

Orleans, he is actually Creed Taylor V, a fact I uncovered after reading that another Creed Taylor had participated in the first battle of the Alamo, when the American forces took the church from the Mexicans. That earlier Creed Taylor —who complained of the way the American forces treated the Mexicans—was a direct ancestor of the present Creed Taylor.

Creed's sandy hair had thinned a little at the back, and he wore slightly tinted glasses after retinal surgery. But he showed no sign of the strain of his eleven-year legal battle with Warner Bros. Records, a battle he won in Santa Monica after the longest civil suit in the history of the California Superior Court.

One thing was different, though: the studio was filled with television equipment, high floodlights shining down from suspended tubes of black cloth and making pools of light on the floor around music stands and microphones, and cameras, including a monstrous instrument mounted on a boom. The crew was getting set up.

Creed won eleven million dollars in that suit; his lawyers had advised him that he could get much more if he wanted to fight further, but he'd said, no, he'd had enough; he wanted to get on with his work, get back to his career, get back to making records. This first session for his CTI label was to be something extraordinary: the first high definition (or hi-def, as it is already being called) jazz video in America and, probably, the world. High-definition television is already on the air an hour a day in Tokyo, and some form of it will probably be in use in America sooner than anyone thinks. With double the number of lines to the screen, it looks like color photos in motion. The vividness is startling. Outside, crews were getting ready for the sessions in a huge video truck next to a generator truck. These cameras were prototypes, and one of them alone was costing Creed $27,000 a day. The mere thought of the cost of this recording made me

uneasy, and only the more so when I mused that this was Creed's own money.

It was a typical Creed Taylor move: daring and original. Like the *Bill Evans with Symphony Orchestra*, which must have been an expensive album; or Bill's three-piano *Conversations with Myself*, which got Bill his first Grammy; or the Freddy Hubbard *Red Clay* album; or *The Individualism of Gil Evans*, made when nobody in the world thought Gil was "commercial" and which Creed made only because he loved Gil's writing. Or the great Jimmy Smith albums. Or the George Benson recordings. Warner Bros. had swiped Benson from Creed, who had a contract with him. That's what he sued them for. And now he was suing CBS records to get back the masters of his CTI records.

Creed had called me in California and asked me to come east and work on this hi-def video project. He wanted me to interview some of the musicians, capture if possible some of their personalities and histories on film in segments to be spaced among the musical numbers. It sounded a little nuts to me, but I have great faith in Creed's imagination. He will take chances, go into things with only a faint idea of how they will come out, putting his faith in the people he's working with. And he had ordered up a varied, to say the least, crew of musicians: among them Art Farmer; Phil Woods; Bob Berg; Anthony Jackson; Charlie Haden; Tito Puente; Airto Moreira and his wife, Flora Purim; and Dizzy Gillespie. Creed idolized Dizzy, still remembering in awe the first time he saw him, fronting his big band back when Creed was an undergraduate in psychology at Duke University. He was looking forward to Dizzy's arrival. And he was treating everyone like royalty.

In the past few days, we had discussed the project at length. Creed said, "How do we keep it out of the record-store bins marked 'various artists'? What's the unifying principle?"

"Dizzy," I said. Because of the breadth of his influence, which goes far beyond bebop. Creed agreed that it certainly was one of the principles. Dizzy was to come in on the last day and record two pieces of material.

Benny Golson and I had been talking about Dizzy in the van on our way out here from Manhattan. We were to pick Art Farmer up on the way. Art lives in Vienna now, and he was staying in the apartment of a friend; Benny had recently moved back to New York after many years of writing film scores in Los Angeles.

"Dizzy was talking about Art last night," Benny said. "Dizzy said, 'Did you hear Art's recording of *U.M.M.G.?*'" I assumed he meant *Upper Manhattan Medical Group*. "The first recording of it I heard was Dizzy's, that he did with Duke. He just happened to come by the studio that day, when they were recording, and he just happened to have his horn. Duke said, 'Take your horn out.' He didn't quite understand the tune, and so Swee'pea, Billy Strayhorn, said, 'Well look, this is the way it goes.' And he played and it was fantastic.

"Dizzy and I talked about an hour on the phone last night. I called him in Atlanta. I told him that many people can follow those who are already taking the lead. But when he came along, he was stepping out into dark places, at some personal risk, I guess—risk of being ridiculed. Louis Armstrong said something like, 'They play like they're playing with a mouthful of hot rice.' Where's the melody? The bass drum is dropping too many bombs. There were all kinds of derogatory things said about them. And now today, it's the standard.

"When John Coltrane and I—we were together every day during that time—went to the Academy of Music to hear Dizzy in 1945, and they started to play, we almost fell off the balcony. Because we had been playing with local bands. And we all were

used to playing . . ." He sang an example of swing era riffing. "And all of a sudden, Dizzy was playing other things, things we had never heard, and you can't imagine the impact it had on me. I told Dizzy last night that that moment changed my whole life, and I've spent the rest of my life trying to comprehend what it's all about. It's so limitless. It's perpetual. Of course, Dizzy is so modest, I could hear the embarrassment coming through the phone."

Benny said, "He was always didactic. Really. He was a teacher without even intending to be. And Art Blakey, too! All of us who came through Art's band, we would do anything for him. Freddy Hubbard and I were talking about that the other day. When I left that band, I was in trouble. I could not play with another drummer. I was irritated, I was annoyed, I would get angry, because I wasn't hearing what I was used to hearing. When I joined his band, I was playing soft, and mellow, and smooth, and syrupy. By the time I left I was playing another way, because I had to. He would do one of those famous four-bar drum rolls going into the next chorus, and I would completely disappear. He would holler over at me, 'Get up out of that hole!'" Benny laughed. "He taught us a lot."

We pulled up in front of a building on the West Side. Art Farmer emerged and we shook hands and embraced. Benny said to him, "Did you bring your box of chops?" Art laughed. Benny explained, "That's Curtis Fuller's line."

"They're on their way. They'll be here by tomorrow," Art said.

We got into the van and the talk turned back to Dizzy. "He makes no claims whatsoever for himself," I said.

"He gets embarrassed," Benny said. "Like a little boy. I was telling Gene about that *U.M.M.G.* thing that he recorded with Duke, and then you recorded. You know, I was talking to Dizzy last night about the time when he and Charlie Parker were together. He said, 'Do you know what Charlie Parker brought? Charlie Parker brought the rhythm. The *way* he played those notes.'"

"The accents," Art said.

"It's the *way* he played it," Benny said. "It was really a combination of the two. I said to him, 'You were so far ahead that when you first recorded, you had Clyde Hart, who was a stride piano player, and Slam Stewart. It took a while for the rest of the instrumentalists to catch up with what you were doing, and the trombone was the last.'"

I said, "Bobby Scott said, 'The rhythm sections were ten years behind Bird and Dizzy.'"

"That's true," Benny said. "They were playing boom-chank boom-chank." Art chuckled. "Art," Benny said, "you know more than I do, because I never really got to know Charlie Parker and you played with him."

"You've seen the movie, I presume," I said.

"I didn't see it," Benny said.

"Yeah," Art said. "I saw it. It didn't get him, but it's not a crime. Because somebody that big, they should either have more input from somebody who knew him, or else do it fifty or a hundred years later. There are too many people around who knew Bird who are disgusted with the movie. If you didn't know him, well then it wouldn't make any difference. And the guy in the picture is nothing like Dizzy. Dizzy is a guy—and Bird was too—when these people walked into the room, you knew there was a presence there. The guy who played the part of Dizzy was very quiet, almost meek, a mousy kind of guy. And Dizzy is nothing like that at all." He and Benny laughed at the discrepancy. "And everyone who knew Bird recognizes that he was very strong intellectually, and had a very strong personality. This guy in the movie came across as somebody who was a little boy, child-like,

and never knew what he was doing. Not to take anything away from the actor—he was a good actor. But he didn't know what he was dealing with. The guy in the movie came across as too much of a victim, a sad guy. Bird had a sense of humor. He wasn't going around crying all the time.

"I remember that when we were living in Los Angeles, there was a little black weekly newspaper called the Los Angeles *Sentinel* that came out with a review of Bird. I read it and I was so surprised that I took it over to where he was staying, and woke him up, and said, 'Hey, man! Read this!' The lady who wrote it said, 'This saxophone player carries himself with the air of a prophet. And he's got a little wispy black boy who plays the trumpet and a bass player with an indefatigable arm.' She said, 'He carries himself with the air of a prophet, but there's really not much going on.' Bird was sitting up in the bed, reading it, and he said, 'Yeah, well, she's probably okay, but the wrong people got to her first.' She was the girlfriend of a trumpet player out there who wasn't into anything."

Benny said, "One of the most ridiculous things I have heard recently was by a female critic who said Kenny G is very much like Charlie Parker. I couldn't believe it. I'm not taking anything away from Kenny G but he's nothing like Charlie Parker.'" And Benny and Art laughed.

For me, too, it was the rhythm in the playing of Charlie Parker and Dizzy Gillespie. Having grown up with Wagner and Debussy and Ravel in my ears, the harmony was not startling. There is little in bebop harmony that wasn't in use in European concert music by the end of the nineteenth century. It was the rhythmic shifting to which Bird and Dizzy were prone that startled me. I had grown up loving Edmond Hall and Trummy Young and George Wettling and Big Sid Catlett and the Goodman small groups, and in them the solos tended to fall into comparatively neat bar divisions, two or compounds of two. Even Coleman Hawkins and Charlie Christian had not prepared me for this swift evolution in jazz. Charlie Parker said once in an interview that he and Dizzy and Don Byas and Kenny Clarke and their friends were not rebelling against anything: they simply thought this was the logical way for the music to go.

I never was able to accept the story that they "invented" bebop at Minton's as a thing the "white boys" couldn't steal. It is at odds with Dizzy's character, his spirituality and unfailing kindness. And anyone who credited that story simply doesn't know how skilled musicians hear. Once I was sitting in Jim and Andy's with Marion Evans, the arranger, when a Les Brown record came on the jukebox. There was a particular smoky sound in the brass that the band occasionally used. I mused vaguely that I wondered what it was. Marion said, "Trumpets voiced in thirds, with trombones doubling in an octave down," and he told me what mutes they were using. He'd never heard the record before. Another time I was at the rehearsal of a large orchestra in Los Angeles, as they prepared to perform Alfred Newman's score for *Captain from Castille* at a concert. There is a particular chord in that music that has always caught my ear, and I expressed my curiosity about it to Dave Raksin, who was standing near me. Dave told what the chord was, its inversion, and spelled it all the way up, including what instruments were on the parts. During World War II, Robert Farnon used to listen to short-wave radio from the U.S., to get the latest pop tunes. He'd write them down as fast they went by, line and changes. I don't hear that well, but I know any number of people who do. The ears of Billy Byers are legendary. So there was no way that, in those early days of bebop, people like Mel Powell or Eddie Sauter or Ray Conniff—any number of people—could be baffled about what was going down on the bandstand at Minton's. In any case, art is never created out of such petty motivations. And if Bird and Dizzy actually didn't want the "white boys" to know what they were doing, why did they so generously show it to people like Stan Levey, Red Rodney, Teddy Kotick, and Al Haig, and hire them to play with them? I hardly ever remember a time when Dizzy didn't have someone white in his group, whether it was Phil Woods in the mid-1950s or, later on, Lalo Schifrin or Mike Longo on piano.

By all reports, Johnny Carisi was always welcome on that Minton's bandstand, because he knew the tunes. If anything—and this was always true in jazz—the idea was to blow anybody off the bandstand who couldn't keep up. One of the men they consistently stomped on was a black tenor player. Dizzy called him the original freedom player—free of melody, free of harmony, and free of time.

Those rhythmic displacements on the first bop records—those starts and stops in funny places in the bar structure, so exciting and surprising finally, weren't what I was used to, and when what Bird and Dizzy were doing began to make sense to me, it was a revelation. My God, such fresh and inventive musical minds.

I first knew Dizzy in 1959, or maybe 1960. I was putting together an article for *Down Beat* that in time took the title *The Years with Yard*. Charlie Parker's nickname was, of course, Yardbird, ultimately shortened by most people to Bird. But I have always heard Dizzy refer to him as Charlie Parker, the name in full, or, sometimes, Yard. Dizzy was playing Minneapolis at the time, and I went up there from Chicago with my photographer friend Ted Williams to take the notes and the pictures for the article that would appear over Dizzy's byline. For some reason now forgotten, we were to meet him in a little park somewhere. As Ted and I approached, we paused to watch him for a minute. Lost in some musical thought, Dizzy was softly dancing, all alone there in the sunlight. I never forgot it; it was one of the most poetic things I have ever seen.

I asked Dizzy about his humor on the bandstand, the jokes, the gestures. He said that if he could do anything to set a sympathetic mood in an audience, for his music, he would do it, and if humor would accomplish that end, he had no intention of giving it up. Even then he was announcing that he would like to introduce the members of his group after which he introduced them all to each other. He still does it. It still gets laughs. But sometimes the humor is quite spontaneous.

Once in the 1970s, he appeared in Los Angeles on a bill with Carmen McRae at a hotel that had decided to "try" a jazz policy. Everything went wrong. The sound system was poor, the piano was out of tune. Part way through Carmen's opening half of the concert, the pedals fell off the piano, and her accompanist was thereafter unable to move well through the chords in her ballads. Dizzy grabbed his horn and rushed on-stage to help her, filling the spaces in her phrases. Intermission came. A crew set up the bandstand for Dizzy's half of the performance.

His microphone stand was high, to pick up the sound of his uptilted horn. But whoever had put it there had left the cord spiralled around the stand. Dizzy came out and looked at it. He shares with the late Jack Benny a curious ability to walk onto a stage and stand there doing absolutely nothing and somehow making the audience laugh. He pretended, as is his wont, that he was unaware that they were there as he examined the problem of the microphone stand. He set his horn on the stage, standing on its bell, its body tilted at a forty-five degree angle. And he studied that mike stand and the cord coiled around it from several angles. The audience had begun to giggle softly. Suddenly he picked it up, held the weighted foot of the stand high in the air, and spun it, so that the cord uncoiled itself. The audience exploded in laughter, and at that point Dizzy affected surprise, as if taken aback by the discovery that he was not alone in the room. He took the mike off the stand, and looked back and forth in mock shock, and then said, "It is twenty years since Charlie Parker and I played Los Angeles." Pause. "It still ain't shit."

The laughter became a roar.

A few years ago, Dizzy changed his embouchure, and now he gets a bigger, fatter tone than he used to. It has acquired a rather velvety quality. I think he paces himself. I doubt that, at seventy-two, he could sustain entire evenings of blazing solos as he did in the late 1940s in front of his big band. But he knows how to handle it.

Someone pointed out to me a while ago that many, perhaps most, of the earlier generation of jazz trumpeters and some of the trombone players sang. Louis Armstrong, Red Allen, Hot Lips Page, Ray Nance, Jack Teagarden, and others would do occasional vocal choruses. Clark Terry still does. Partly it was because they were a generation that considered they were in show business, they were there to entertain. But I suspect they did it as well as a way to rest their chops. I heard Dizzy in a university concert in Chicago a year or two ago. He played superbly. And then he did two numbers in which he didn't play at all. He clowned a little, and sang—one of the numbers being, inevitably, *Swing Low, Sweet Cadillac*. And then he went into the closing number, a long burning solo at a fast tempo. He was at the absolute peak of his form, full of surprises, simple melodic phrases alternating with those cascades of notes. And I concluded he had sung those two tunes to give his lip time to rest up for this finale.

He is, aside from being one of the major figures in modern musical history, a very shrewd showman.

The first day of the session was devoted to setting up the sound and the cameras. The musicians ran the material down. Phil Woods had been engaged for the session, but he was on his way back from Europe and Jerry Dodgion subbed for him. The material Benny had written was tough, and Creed realized it was going to be hard on Art Farmer's lip. He wanted Art more for his solo value than as a lead player, and set Amy Landon, his assistant, to checking on several potential players to ease Art's burden. There is a softness about Creed that causes him to be very reserved, as if to protect himself from the importuning world; I once took it for coldness. I was wrong.

The summer of 1989 was viciously hot in the northern east coast United States. It rained every second day, at most every third day, and the humidity between rains was almost unendurable, particularly in Manhattan. Those powerful television lights completely overcame the air conditioning in Rudy's studio and turned it into a sauna.

We were all drained at the end of the day, when I rode back to the Omni Park hotel—where Creed had put most of us up—with Airto Moreira and his wife, Flora Purim. Flora reminded me of something: that when she and Airto arrived in New York from Brazil in the mid-1960s, they stayed in my apartment for a week or so until they found a place of their own. I had completely forgotten about it.

The van crossed the George Washington Bridge. The buildings of Manhattan receded to the south in layers of aerial perspective, at last to disappear in the pale humidity.

Airto said, "We were in Europe for two weeks at Ronnie Scott's club with our band, every night, two sets, very late—we would start at 10:45 p.m., first set, second set one o'clock to two something. We did that for two weeks, then we went all over Europe for almost three weeks with Dizzy Gillespie and an all-star United Nations band. So it was pretty heavy: flying every day, waking up at 6:30 in the morning, going to the airport, the plane leaves at nine, baggage outside the room at six o'clock. Got my luggage stolen, two big bags."

Flora said, "It was great working with Dizzy. Dizzy is one of the greatest teachers, without teaching you. He shows you ways of handling life. When he goes onstage, and the music changes, it's so easy, so humorous. Everything is a laugh, it's fun, and if it's not fun, he doesn't want to do it. He's been a big inspiration to us lately. The last year, we've been working on and off with him.

"We're losing a lot of players who are the center, and Dizzy Gillespie is one of the last of them. If Dizzy hadn't come up with his bebop, we wouldn't be here."

Airto said, "He made the fusion of Latin music and jazz. He was the first one who understood it and tried to play with those guys, and did it."

"He's still doing it," Flora said. "Dizzy is still behind the fusion of Latin and jazz music."

Airto said, "He just blew our minds on the road for three weeks in Europe. Flying every day, as I said. We were so tired, we couldn't even rehearse the sound anymore. Dizzy would just come in and play, and then everybody felt good, and thinking if this man is playing like this, at least we should play *something*. And very strong. I don't know how he does that, at seventy-two."

Flora said, "His energy level is very high, and what he stands behind is very strong, even though he's very shy to say it. We've done some interviews together, and sometimes people would ask him why he was still doing it, and he would come off with things like, 'For the money.' Which is not true. He doesn't need the money at all. He's a rich man."

"He's made some good money," Airto said.

"He's there," Flora said, "because this is life. This is life to him, and to us. There are different kinds of musicians. There are musicians who make their livelihood emotionally, not just financially. I believe Dizzy is one of them. Art Blakey is another one of them. We look up to them as examples."

The next morning, I rode out to Rudy's with Phil Woods, who'd just got in, and was weary. In Paris, he and Dizzy and a number of other American jazz musicians had been honored by the government of France. Phil's wife, Jill Goodwin—she's the sister of Bill Goodwin, Phil's drummer; and they are the children of announcer Bill Goodwin, whom older readers will remember from the network radio days—said to me once, "Phil's angry at all the right things." It's a remarkably apt description.

Phil said: "Just come back from Paris where François Mitterand presented Milt Jackson, myself, Stan Getz, Jackie McLean, Percy Heath with medals, made us *Officiers* of the Order of Arts and Letters, which is one step above the *Chevalier*, and Dizzy had already been named Chevalier and Officier, so he was named Commandant. It was neat, man. Danielle, the president's wife, a lovely lady, came to two concerts. Some cats were saying that she understood the changes, she was singing along. She loves *A Night in Tunisia* and all that stuff.

"I was trying to relate that to my country, Bush coming up with a polka band or something.

"But how wild. You go to France and they recognize American jazz. It was kind of neat. I'll show you the medal." He pulled it out, displaying it in its velvet-lined case. "I wore it all the way home on the plane. It didn't impress customs at all. Isn't that something? I got a lot of salutes from the police in France. It

helps with your parking tickets. This and two dollars will get you a beer at Jim and Andy's. It's amazing, isn't it, how other cultures accept our music so readily, and here, it's hard to get arrested?"

"Where did you first meet Dizzy?" I asked.

"I met Dizzy in 1956, when we did a State Department tour, first stop Abadan, Iran; next stop Aleppo, Syria; Damascus, Bayreuth. All the trouble spots, all the places that are now on fire, the State Department sent Dizzy. I think if they'd sent him one more time, he could have cooled it all out. But obviously the State Department knew something. That's what always bugs me. When there's trouble in the world, our government recognizes jazz. But the rest of the time, we have troubles with the subsidies and all that. We get the roach, what's left over. The National Endowment for the Arts disseminates huge amounts of money. A category called Folk, Ethnic, and Jazz splits about ten or twenty million—a pittance. Most of the money goes for blue-haired ladies listening to Mahler, conducted by some cat from Israel or somewhere else. You go to France and they give you medals, and wine, and dine you, and treat you like an artist.

"I was with Dizzy for the Mideast tour, and then South America. I had known Dizzy before, but only peripherally. When you work with him, you get to know him. But going to Iran first, that was a killer. And they loved the music. They didn't understand the jazz part, but Dizzy has such an important thing. The rhythm, that grabs people immediately. If you don't know anything about bebop. Dizzy is such a master of rhythm, the Afro, the South American. He was the first cat to fuse the jazz and the Cuban and the South American. Dizzy is the cat who discovered that, the first cat who used conga drums and all that, with Chano Pozo. That's a real big contribution of Diz, which is sometimes overlooked—not by musicians, of course. A lot of people know about the bebop part, but not the rhythm. He loves to play drums.

"When we were in the Mideast, he was out there playing with snake charmers. He'll sit in anywhere—Carnival in Rio, any drummer, any rhythm. he has an uncanny ability to memorize it or feel exactly what they're doing, and then fitting it into the jazz mode, without prostituting either one of them. He's a rhythmic genius.

"That stick he carries—did you ever see that, that thing he made out of a stick and Coca-Cola bottle-caps?"

"Yes, I have. In fact, I suggested to Creed that he use it as a visual motif. He called Dizzy, and Dizzy had lost it, so Creed had one made for him." There's no name for this instrument of Dizzy's invention. It is a pole with a rubber pad on the bottom. He mounted bottle caps on nails on a stick. He can stand in a room and bounce that thing and kick it with his toe and stomp a beat with his foot or shake this thing in the air, setting up the damnedest swing you ever heard, all by himself. I just call it Dizzy's rhythm stick.

Phil said, "I once flew back with him on the Concorde. When you travel with Dizzy, it's incredible. He was carrying that stick, right through the metal detector at the airport. The detector flips out with a hundred Coca-Cola caps rattling. And all the control people cheer and applaud: here comes Dizzy with that silly thing! The big stick. He plays it all the way through the airport; you can hear him come a mile away. He gets away with it."

"There was time," I said, "when we all thought nobody in other countries could play jazz, but not anymore."

"No no," Phil said. "That's no longer true at all."

I reminded him of the group he once led, during his long residence in France, called The European Rhythm Machine.

He said, "We used to call it The European Washing Machine.

The cleanest band in the West. Look at the people you've got today. Neils-Henning Ørsted Pederson. All the way back to Django Reinhardt, Grappelli, René Thomas, Daniel Humair. The list is long. They used to say that horn players were okay, but the line went that the drummers didn't swing, the rhythm sections were inferior to ours. That's no longer the case. It's all over now. There are some Japanese bands that sound great. There's a cat in Japan who copies Miles so closely that when Miles fired his piano player, he fired *his* piano player in Japan. And the jazz clubs of Russia are flourishing."

A few days before this, the crackdown on the Tiananmen Square protesters had begun, and the executions were under way. Phil said, "We were supposed to go to China, but I told my agent to cancel the tour—I'd love to go to China. My band is a natural, since we don't use microphones. We're not a fusion band. We play Porter, Gershwin, and what have you. But for the moment I think we'll hold back on that. That's about the only country I've missed."

We reached Rudy's. Phil and Art Farmer embraced. Art told us a story. Some years ago, late at night, Grady Tate had left Baron's in Harlem. As he was getting into his car, a man pointed a gun at him and demanded his money. Grady emptied his wallet and handed the money over. The man said, "Hey, ain't you Grady Tate?"

Grady admitted that he was.

The holdup man said, "Hey, I've got all your classics."

Grady said, "I've got a new album. I've got some in the back. I'll give you some."

The man said, "No, that's cool, man. I'll buy my own."

Phil and Art and Benny and the others went into the studio and began to rehearse. The tenor player was Bob Berg, from

Brooklyn. His playing was hot, hard, and beautiful. Flora and the band rehearsed a complex piece by Gilberto Gil called *Quilombo*, which called for her to spit out the words at incredible speed and make them swing. She did it, too, and I was astonished by her. Astonished, too, by how much she had grown since Creed and I first heard her in the 1960s. Airto was cooking all over his complex of rhythm instruments, some of which he invented, working closely with Tito Puente. Airto's beard is now flecked with grey; Tito's full head of curly hair is now white. I talked to him during the lunch break, as most of the musicians and the crew gathered at trestle tables in the shadows of trees to consume the catered food Creed had laid on for them. Though Tito speaks fluent Spanish, his English is without accent—or rather, it is that of New York City.

"When I went to Juilliard," Tito said, as leaf-shadows made by a hazy sun played on his handsome face, "I came from the navy. I was in the navy during the war. They paid for the lessons. I went to study arranging and composition and conducting—not percussion. Nothing to do with Latin music. I went to the old school, the one that was on Manhattan Avenue at 124th Street.

"I studied trap drumming when I was seven years old. In the neighborhood in which I lived, in Spanish Harlem, there was a band that I used to sit in with, and a man named Montecino, who is still alive, showed me how to play the timbales. I already had the execution of the drumming, and that helped me to get into the timbales, which I'm very happy I did now.

"Dizzy was probably the first one to bring the Latin rhythms into jazz—with Chano Pozo. That was '46 or '47. His was the first big jazz orchestra to really utilize these Latin rhythms. Then after that we had Stan Kenton and Duke Ellington, and Woody Herman. I wrote some charts for Woody Herman and we did an album together. I've known Dizzy forty years or more—not longer than Mario Bauza, of course.

"The band that really started what we now call Latin jazz was the great Machito, who passed away about five years ago. He developed the influences of Cuba, Haiti, Santo Domingo, Puerto Rico, and Brazil.

"I grew up with a lot of drummers around me in Spanish Harlem. That's where I learned a lot about the rhythms, thanks to Machito—he was my mentor—and Mario Bauza, who is still around today and is one of the greatest maestros of our music and knows everything about the Cuban music. He's responsible for a lot of our music being played today."

Mario Bauza plays a significant role in the life of Dizzy Gillespie. Born in Havana in 1911, he is one of the many refutations of the idea that jazz and classical music have always been separate and unrelated streams. He played bass clarinet in the Havana Symphony Orchestra, and then, after moving to the United States, played trumpet with Chick Webb, Don Redman and Cab Calloway. It was Bauza who brought Dizzy into the Cab Calloway band, where his national reputation began to catch hold. That was in 1939, a year before Dizzy met Charlie Parker in Kansas City, and we may assume that Dizzy, then twenty-two, was introduced to the rhythms of Caribbean music at least that far back.

Later that afternoon, during a break, I heard Romero Lubambo, an excellent young guitarist from Brazil, talking to one of the camera crew. He is tall, with a full face and sandy hair. He said, "The whole time I was in Brazil, I liked to listen to American musicians to learn how to improvise, how to play jazz. Now I am playing with the greatest musicians in the world, I think. For me it is fantastic. We used a lot of the American know-how of doing jazz improvising. What I did in Brazil, and what I am doing here, is playing Brazilian music together with the American. For me it is very close, American and Brazilian. Jazz is very influential in Brazilian music and vice versa.

"Until thirty years ago, we didn't have many improvising in Brazilian music. I'm not so old, but it was singing. But not with many improvisation, and then we borrowed the jazz know-how. This is from what I understand.

"Dizzy through his seventy-something years made everybody be happy when they heard his name. Everybody here is happy already, to see him tomorrow. Everybody is looking forward to seeing him laughing and playing, always great. It's nice."

At Newark Airport the next morning, I waited. Dizzy was playing an engagement in Washington, and flying in for one afternoon of this three-day recording. I was thinking about Dizzy's essential character, about the title of one of his finest tunes, "Con Alma," which is Spanish, meaning with feeling or with soul. It is a wonderfully appropriate title for a tune by Dizzy.

How did this boy, with that curiously elegant natal name John Birks Gillespie, son of a father who abused and beat him in his childhood, who grew up in a society that committed unspeakable acts of racism all around him, and many of them upon him and on his friend Charlie Parker, grow up to be so loving? It has always seemed to me a triumph of the human spirit that anyone born black in America can even bear the company of white people, and for Dizzy, who years ago took up the Baha'i religion, to have such love for his fellow man amounts to a miracle. It is not that he is unmindful of the abuses of his people. But he has found laughter even in that. Lalo Schifrin, who

was his pianist in the early 1960s, told me of walking up a street with Dizzy in Glasgow or Edinburgh. Occasionally, affecting that very proper English he can turn on or off at will, he would stop someone on the street and say, "Pardon me, my name is Gillespie, and I'm looking for my relatives." He would leave some baffled Scot looking after him as Lalo fell apart with laughter.

His antic humor has been part of his life apparently since he was very young. It dates at least as far back as his early twenties, when he was working in a band in Philadelphia, because someone there named him Dizzy. He no longer remembers who put the name on him, "but," he says, "I'm glad he did." I first heard of him when he got fired from the Cab Calloway band, purportedly for firing spitballs at Cab. But that not only illuminates his life offstage: it is used very shrewdly onstage. One of my most vivid memories is of an incident in which his laughter, his clowning, his shrewd showmanship, and above all his kindness, came together on a stage in Canada.

It happened this way.

I was asked to do an evening of my songs at one of a series of concerts sponsored by the Canadian Broadcasting Corporation at a place called Camp Fortune in the Gatineau Hills, outside Ottawa. I was told I could use a large orchestra, which meant arrangements had to be written. I chose Chico O'Farrill to write them, because I love his work, and we were neighbors and friends. When Chico agreed to do the concert, the producer, Peter Shaw, asked him to perform his Aztec Suite. It had been written for and recorded by Art Farmer. Peter asked us to track Art down and ask if he would join us in the concert, but Art had moved to Europe and we had trouble finding him. Chico said, "How about Dizzy?"

And I said, "Why not? We can always ask him."

We called Dizzy and he agreed to do it—which meant that he had to read and learn a by no means simple piece of music in one or two rehearsals. But this presented me with a problem. I am essentially a writer, not a performer. Performance takes certain highly honed skills that I lack. And there is no more brilliant *performer*, questions of music aside, than Dizzy. I told Peter, "There is absolutely no way I'm going to follow Dizzy Gillespie on a stage. I'll open; he can close." But, Peter suggested, this would set up an imbalance. So Chico and I wrote a new song, in long form, that we could do with Dizzy as a closer.

Dizzy, as it happened, got delayed by weather in St. Louis and missed the first rehearsal. Chico rehearsed the orchestra, with Mike Renzi playing the trumpet part in transposition on the piano, no mean feat in itself. Dizzy got there in time for the final rehearsal, and seemed to be memorizing the *Aztec Suite* as fast as he was reading. That was the afternoon I came to appreciate his consummate musicianship, questions of jazz quite apart.

Well, the evening came, and terrified or not, I sang my half of the concert, apparently not disastrously. The audience was warm, and at the end I said something to the effect that I had never before sung my lyrics in the country in which I was born, and I was very glad to be there. Then I said something like, "Now, ladies and gentlemen, it is my privilege to introduce one of the great musicians of our time, Mr. Dizzy Gillespie."

Birks came out on the stage, looking (as is his wont) as if he was startled to find people there—and there were five or ten thousand of them, I would guess, blanketing the hillside of a natural amphitheater in front of the stage. He took the mike from the stand, gave a long Jack Benny pause, and said, "Damn! I'm glad I'm a Canadian!" The audience roared, and as usual he had them in his hand before he'd played a note. And then he and Chico and the orchestra sailed into the *Aztec Suite*.

He played brilliantly—this piece he had never played before.

There is a gesture he has, a motion, that always reminds me of a great batter leaning into a hit. He has a way of throwing one foot forward, putting his head down a bit as he silently runs the valves, and then the cheeks boom out in the way that has mystified his dentist for years, and he hits into the solo. When that foot goes forward like that, you know that John Birks Gillespie is no longer clowning. Stand back.

And that foot went forward a lot that night. At the end of the suite, the audience went crazy. They were screaming. Backstage I said to Peter Shaw, "I'm not going out into that. I'm not that nuts."

But Chico and the orchestra and Dizzy were setting up for the number I was to do with them. Now Dizzy's part was a long one, written out on accordion-folded music paper. He started to put it on his music stand and dropped it. It spilled at his feet, and the audience tittered a little. Setting his horn down on its bell, he got down on his knees and started to fold it, like a man trying to put a road-map back the way he found it. When he had it neatly together, he stood up; and dropped it a second time. He did this three times, until Chico and the orchestra and the audience and I were helpless with laughter and the mood at the end of the *Aztec Suite* had faded into the past. He let the laughter die down. And then he introduced me. He handed that audience to me. I couldn't believe the generosity of this; or the cleverness, the canny sense of show.

And we finished the concert and went to a party. It was probably that night that he told me he had never in life walked onto a stage without feeling at least a little nervous, and that humor helped to break the feeling.

I got thinking about the last time I'd seen Birks. We'd been guests on one of Steve Allen's TV shows in Los Angeles. Three of these shows were shot that day. We were on the first of them, and one guest on the second show was to be Doc Severinsen.

Dizzy said he wanted to stick around after we'd finished and hear Doc play. One of the girls in makeup heard him say it, and passed it along to Doc. I heard Doc reply, "Oh boy! That's all I *need*—Dizzy Gillespie listening to me." A little later he came to our dressing room, and Dizzy greeted him warmly, and they fell immediately into the camaraderie of men in the same profession. They didn't talk about music. They talked about lip salves and medications. Birks said, "I've got something great! Freddy Hubbard turned me onto it."

He opened his trumpet case and gave a small package to Doc. "Try it," he said.

It came time for Doc to do his show. Dizzy stood in the shadows, listening. Doc played with a small group. There were none of the high notes, none of the flourishes, you hear during his usual television appearances. He played a ballad, mostly in middle register, the notes sparse and thoughtfully selected. He sounded a lot like, of all people, Bix Beiderbecke. "He's beautiful," Dizzy said, and if Doc in the spotlight had been able to see the smile of John Birks Gillespie in the shadows, he would have felt compensated for all the dismissals of his jazz playing by critics.

I have a very deep love for Dizzy Gillespie. He has contributed immeasurable joy to our troubled era. And to me, he has contributed insight.

These thoughts were in my mind as he got off the plane, carrying the big, square, black case that accommodates his idiosyncratic trumpet, and wearing sandals and a short-sleeved safari jacket.

He grinned, greeted the driver of the van and our cameraman and sound technician, and got into the back seat. I was in the front seat, leaning over its back, and I suddenly had a wave of emotion. "Hey Birks," I said, "I'm awful glad to see you."

He went serious. He tapped the middle of his chest, indicating his heart. His goatee is grey now, and so is his head. He said, "Me . . . too!"

I told him Creed had ordered a new version of his rhythm stick made for him; Dizzy had misplaced the last one, made with pop-bottle caps. This one was deluxe, made not with bottle caps but the tiny cymbals you find in tambourines. I said it was at the studio, waiting for him. "Where'd you find that thing originally?" I said.

"I made the first one," he said, and I remembered the first time I'd seen it. He demonstrated it to Jerome Richardson and me, and we were astonished at the polyrhythms he could set up with it. "I made two or three after that." He chuckled. His voice is low and a little thick in its texture, with a touch of the south in its accent. He is one jazz musician whose speech is not like his playing; in fact they are radically different. "That stick was something. I could be at one end of the airport and be walking with that stick, and all the guys knew where I was, from the rattle. Every now and then I would do it, and they'd know where to find me."

I said, "Everybody I've talked to, Phil Woods, Benny Golson, Art Farmer, said you have always been the great teacher. I remember Nat Adderley said once, 'Dizzy's the greatest teacher in the world if you don't let him know he's doing it.'"

"Is that true? I don't know about that," he said, and I saw that embarrassment Benny Golson had described. This was no affectation of modesty; this was genuine humility. "But what little I do know, I'll give it, any time. So I guess it's not actually someone with a whole lot of knowledge giving it out to people. But anything I learned, I'll tell somebody else. So that's what they mean by that. I will tell anything that I've learned."

"Miles said to me once, 'I got it all from Dizzy.' Art Farmer said that you came in to hear him one night and he realized that everything he was playing, he'd learned from you."

"That's a good question, about those guys. One example is Art Farmer," he said, trying to steer the conversation away from himself. "I made a record with Duke, a Duke Ellington party. I wasn't called to make the record, but I just went by the record date to see all the guys in the band I hadn't seen in some time. And when I walked in, Duke pulled out this *U.M.M.G.*, and said, 'I want you to try this.' So he gave me the part and they played it. And then Strayhorn was there. Strayhorn had to show me a couple of things. There were some very big surprises in that number—the resolutions at certain parts. Out of a clear blue sky, boom! A-flat minor seventh. And how it got there, you don't know. So Strayhorn came over to the piano and showed me and then I didn't have any trouble.

"But Art Farmer!" The sound of South Carolina was in the way he said it: Aht Fahmuh. Driving in South Carolina two or three years ago, I was slightly startled by a sign on the highway that indicated the direction to Cheraw. It looked so matter of fact. I vaguely thought it should say under the name: Birthplace of John Birks Gillespie. "Boy!" Dizzy said. "I heard Art Farmer do it. I just happened to have the radio on, and boy! This guy! He must have spent some time on this number, because he knew every in and out of the progressions, he knew all of the resolutions. Boy, he really operated on that. Like a surgeon. Art Farmer is some fantastic musician. He's so pretty. Some guys can play all the changes, and you don't get the significance of the resolutions going from one to the other. But Art Farmer, he's so gentle. Just beautiful. I'm sorry I made the number. But if I hadn't made the number, Art wouldn't have made it, because he liked the record I made with Duke, and he said, 'I want some of that,' and he went and got it.

"Art Farmer. Nat Adderley. There's some good trumpet players around. I think there are more than in the early days.

Because we had a hard core of young trumpet players, like Charlie Shavers, Kenny Dorham, Fats Navarro, and of course Miles is in there and, let's see—Dud Bascomb. He was a very tasty trumpet player. We used to talk when I was at the Savoy with Teddy Hill's band and Dud was with Erskine Hawkins. We used to say, 'Man! I wonder what it would be to be with someone like Duke Ellington and Cab Calloway.' And he wound up with Duke Ellington and I went with Cab Calloway. So we got two of the best jobs in New York. But that Dud Bascomb!

"And then there was a trumpet player named Little Willie, who played Buddy Johnson. He was very talented, too. He didn't get a chance to play too much on records."

"Birks, I want to talk to you about the Caribbean, and the Afro-Cuban, and the Brazilian. It's like Phil Woods and others say, you were the first jazz musician to get into that music, to combine jazz with these various Latin influences."

"And I'll tell you something," Dizzy said, "the Latin guys play jazz better than guys play Latin." That was something to think about.

He said, "I was always interested in that music. All of my compositions have a Latin tinge. Every one of them. And that means that I am a lover of Latin music. I remember the first time I went to Argentina, I composed a piece that sounded like their music, called *Tango-rene*. I recorded it with the big band. That was a nice trip. I like Argentina very much.

"This year I was in Budapest. In my hotel they had a gypsy band, with a guy who played violin. He was *bad*, boy. I was supposed to come back after our performance in the theater and play a little bit with them. But that's where the tango comes from—that area of the gypsies.

"Which reminds me of a time in Africa. I went to Kenya for the State Department for the tenth anniversary of independence for Kenya. They took me to a dance one night. And I heard these guys playing. And I closed my eyes, and it sounded like calypso, the West Indian guys. So when the musicians asked me how I liked the music, I said, 'To tell you the truth, it sounded very similar to West Indian music.' And one of the guys, he say, 'You know, we were here first!' I said, 'Thank you very much.'" And he laughed at the memory.

I asked him what caused that immediate affinity between them when he first heard Charlie Parker in Kansas City, during his time with Cab Calloway.

"The method and music impressed me, the more I heard him play. Because it was so much the way that I thought music should go. His style! The style! Was perfect for our music. I was playing like Roy Eldridge at the time. In about a month's time, I was playing like Charlie Parker. From then on—maybe adding a little here and there. But Charlie Parker was the most fantastic . . . I don't know. You know, he used to do tunes inside of tunes. He'd be playing something and all of sudden you'd hear *I'm in the Mood for Love* for four bars. Or two bars. Lorraine told me one time, 'Why don't you play like Charlie Parker?' I said, 'Well, that's Charlie Parker's style. And I'm not a copyist of someone else's music.' But he was the most fantastic musician."

When we got to Rudy van Gelder's, the camera crew asked Dizzy to wait a few minutes so they could get shots of his arrival. He waited a little, then began to get impatient. He said he wanted to get out and warm up his lip. He waited some more, finally got out, and went directly into the studio, where Benny Golson was rehearsing one of the numbers Dizzy was to record. Everything stopped, and the mood in the place became reverent. Various of the musicians shook his hand, or hugged him, and he wore that great embracing grin. Art Farmer beamed; his hair, too, is gray now. Phil Woods, in a red polo shirt and a small leather cap, grinned, and shook hands. "Sky King," he said. It's his nickname for Dizzy, because he is always in an airplane, going from one gig to another. In fact, though he lived only a short walk from this studio, he wouldn't even have time to go home to see his wife, Lorraine, before flying back to Washington later today.

"Hey!" Dizzy said, when he saw the rhythm stick Creed had had made for him. "Beautiful!" And he gave it a few experimental shakes.

He left the studio, went out to one of the trailers that were standing by, took out his horn, and began to practice. After a while he came back, and the recording began. Dizzy played on two tunes, both Latin and both rhythmically powerful. In each case he mastered the material quickly and soared off into solos, the notes cascading down from his horn. The takes were interrupted repeatedly. What began to be apparent is that the compound rhythms weren't bothering Dizzy, but the polyrhythms he was piling on top of them were bothering the band. One tune, "Wamba," kept breaking down at the same point, and Benny Golson, in a red shirt, would start it again. Dizzy's every solo was totally fresh, unrelated in any way to his solos in the previous takes. The studio grew hotter. Dizzy opened the safari jacket and played bare-chested, always with that uncanny concentration he brings to bear.

The rhythm . . . the rhythm!

I was in the booth with Creed and Rudy; I couldn't bear the heat of the studio, and didn't know how the musicians were doing so. Dizzy kept playing. "That man is a miracle of neurological organization." I said to Creed.

"That's a good way to put it," Creed said.

The tune kept breaking down; I kept looking at the clock. This was the last day of shooting, with that one camera alone at

$27,000 a day. . . . And Dizzy had to return late in the afternoon to Washington. There could be no extensions of the date. The suspense was getting to me. Creed showed nothing; not a flicker of anxiety. He is always like that. I don't know how he does it. Maybe the training in psychology . . .

And at last it was over. Dizzy did his two brilliant takes. The musicians applauded. Creed went into the studio to thank him. Dizzy packed up his horn. A limousine took him back to the airport.

I said to Creed, who is never ever demonstrative, "Well, are you happy?"

"No," he said with a trace of a smile. "I'm ecstatic."

All the musicians were packing up. Soon the studio was empty. Across a chair lay Dizzy's rhythm stick, the new one Creed had had made, and that Dizzy loved. Creed planned to send it over to his house, a minor gift. The light from above flooded the stick, Dizzy's music stand and the microphone, set high for his uptilted horn. It was as if the ghost of this colossus were still there.

Throughout those days, I was forcefully struck by the diversity of America that is represented in jazz. When I was a teenager, listening to bands and dazzled by the solos of Ray Nance, Cootie Williams, and so many others, some of them—Zoot Sims, for example—not much older than I, I wondered if this music was just a job to them, one that got boring from doing it night after night, or if it was a genuine passion.

I learned very early that it is the latter.

Charlie Haden said it as well as I have ever heard it expressed after the last session.

He said: "It's very rare in the recording industry for a producer to place such importance on creative values. Jazz, for so many years, has been treated as a tax write-off for most big record companies. And now, more and more, conglomerate corporations that are in the record business are just looking to sell many many records and make a lot of hits and a lot of money. Which is okay, but it's kind of sad that the art forms and the deeper values are forgotten about.

"That's sad for the jazz musician, and other artists dedicated to their art forms, film-making, poetry, dance, painting."

"I feel it is the responsibility of every one of us to improve the quality of life; to make this planet a better place; to bring deeper values back to the society, which are taken away from the people by the conditioning of mass media, of society's profit-oriented racist-sexist values. People are taught by the mass media what they should like, what they should wear, what they should listen to. And then they are sold these things.

"It's very sad that this music is put on the side, and not many people know about the importance of this art form we call jazz. And the other sad thing is that whenever someone has an opportunity to educate people in film about this art form, they always miss the mark. They never show the brilliance or improvisation and what it really is. They show a romantic story, or a story about drugs, or a story about alcohol, or the perennial image of the jazz musician as a child who hasn't grown up; who cares only about sex and alcohol and drugs and music, and really doesn't have any feelings or opinions or ideas or interests about any other things in life. Which is very sad, because it's not true.

"I think that Creed has done a great thing here, by making this record and also making it a video, so that people can see what we're all about, and what we love, and why we're doing what we're doing: we're actually fulfilling a calling to a responsibility to the universe. And that is to make beautiful music, and bring beauty and deeper values to people's lives, so that they can touch the deeper parts inside themselves. And there will be more of us.

"If the leaders of all the countries of the world were able to sit down and think about these things and to bring this music and these values to the people of the world, there would be a different mentality. The governments of different countries would be concerned about life. They would have reverence for life, instead of placing importance on weapons.

"It's all included in this music, the beauty of all those things. Because improvisation teaches you the magic of being in the moment you're living in. You get a different perspective about life. And you see yourself in relation to the universe in a completely different way. There's no such thing as yesterday, there's no such thing as tomorrow. They're only right now, when you're improvising. The spontaneity is there. When you're touching music, you see your extreme unimportance.

"The reason it hasn't been given more to the public, there's no vested interest, there's no profit being made. Since the beginning of this country, if there's no profit being made, they won't give it to the people.

"That's why government subsidy is really difficult. In Europe, you have a lot of countries that subsidize jazz concerts and musicians. It doesn't happen in the United States and it's very sad. The only thing that is similar to subsidization is the National Endowment for the Arts, which isn't nearly enough.

"People should be able to turn on television and see beautiful music. If I were an alien from another planet, and I landed in Queens one night, and I walked to the nearest house and looked in the windows and I saw the kids sitting on the floor, looking at MTV, I would say to myself, 'My God, is this the best that this country's popular artists have? Are these the best values they have to give to their young people?'

"Values of sequins, limousines, wealth, perpetuated every day with the whole superstar structure of the music industry. And every time that you bring music with deep values to people, it touches somebody.

"It's the people who have corrupted the music that we have to worry about, that we have to try and change, and one of the ways of doing this is to just keep playing, and to present the music to as many people as possible, because the more people hear this music, the more people are going to be attracted to it.

"And, hopefully, more endeavors will happen like we just did, because it brings great musicians together who usually don't have a chance to play music with each other, and it allows them to feel comfortable and relaxed in improvisation. And, when music is presented on the same level that the music is played, that's the thing that's really meaningful. When it's presented on a level of reverence and respect.

"People have lost their appreciation for beauty. The great thing about this art form is that musicians care about beautiful sound. They want to make their instruments sound really really beautiful. It's so important, beautiful sound—to be able to hear the beauty of the musician's soul. Every musician . . . they learn their favorite notes, they discover their favorite notes, their favorite sound, and they make their music sound as beautiful as they can for the listener, and that's what makes it so great. It's a dedication and an honesty that you don't find very many places. Improvisation and spontaneity are about honesty. It's completely pure honesty. The musician is baring his soul to the people, and hoping he can touch their lives, in a humble way. Every great musician learns that before they can become a great musician, they have to become a good human being. That's the important thing, to strive to be a good human being, and to have humility.

"It's like the guy in Washington a few years ago. In the middle of winter, an airliner crashed in the middle of the Potomac River. People were on their way home from work. A guy got out of his car. He saw a woman who got out of the aircraft and couldn't reach the lifeline that was being thrown to her. And he didn't think twice, he jumped into the river and rescued her, and disappeared. Finally someone found him and said, 'What's your name?' And he said, 'It doesn't matter what my name is, I just did what I had to do.'

"And that's greatness to me."


I got up early the next morning in the hotel and called Phil Woods. Phil and his wife had found me a house for the summer near their own. They live in Delaware Water Gap, Pennsylvania. We got into the car. Phil told me the best way was to go out through the Lincoln Tunnel. I hate the New York tunnels. They give me what Woody Herman used to call the clausters. I'm always afraid the roof is going to fall in and, New York being what is has become, probably some day it will. I wanted to go out over the George Washington Bridge.

Phil said the other route was faster. "Only take us an hour and twenty minutes or so."

"You sure?"

"Promise," he said.

But the whole West Side was tied up with traffic because President George Bush was coming to New York for some event or another. And when we got down in the tunnel, the traffic stopped completely.

"Hey, Phil, you promised me," I said.

"It'll be cool," he said.

At last it crawled forward. But hardly had we come out of the tunnel than it stopped cold again on the highway. People shut off their engines and got out and stood around on the cement. I asked a truck driver who had climbed to the roof of his cab to look ahead what was happening. "Ah the president's coming in or something," he said.

Of course. From Newark airport, where I'd picked up Dizzy the day before. The air was as hot and humid as ever. Phil and I stood around on the highway and told music business stories. We were there a half hour or so. The truck driver said, "Next time, I'm voting Democrat!"

And then, on a parallel highway, we saw it, the cavalcade of black limousines with dark glass, the one with the pennant identifying the president's car. How silly. To tie up this traffic like this. Why didn't they fly him in a helicopter to the Pan Am building? What was all this gasoline costing? I wondered if the man in that dark car would ever recognize the contribution of Dizzy Gillespie to the American culture; it seemed unlikely. And if he ever did, it would be for political reasons.

The traffic started moving again; we'd been on our way for an hour and a half. "Phil, you said an hour and twenty minutes!"

Inevitably, we talked more about Dizzy. "The Sky King," Phil said again.

I said, "I think his sense of humor lets him get away with things the rest of us wouldn't have the nerve to try."

"You know, " Phil said, "he didn't do any clowning at all on this European trip. Occasionally he likes to do jokes and sing and scat. But when we did the All Star thing, which was Hank Jones, Max Roach, Stan Getz, Jackie McLean, Milt Jackson, boy was he playing. Because he knew he was with the musicians who grew up with him, and there was no funny business. He was all serious, man. Some European critics have said, ah, Dizzy's chops are gone. I hope they were there that night." Phil whistled. "He was hitting high R's."

"Dizzy changed the way of the world. That music means so much to so many people everywhere."

Phil searched the radio dial until he found a jazz station. We heard a superb pianist whom we could not identify. It turned out to be Kenny Barron. The sky darkened. We were in a cloudburst. I slowed to about thirty miles an hour as the sheets of rain swept across the highway and all the crawling cars turned their head- lights on. We'd been traveling now more than two and a half hours.

"Phil, you promised me!"

And the sun came out.

# *Dizzy*

*Danny Barker and Dizzy Gillespie on the road with the Cab Calloway Band, 1940. Photograph © Milton J. Hinton.*

"Diz was a kid when he joined Cab's band in the late '30s. Many guys in the band laughed at his playing, but a few of us who listened recognized that he was way ahead of his time. He was always willing to share his knowledge. Sometimes when we worked the Cotton Club and the weather was warm, the two of us would take our instruments up to the roof during intermissions. He'd show me some of his chord inventions and get me to try new ways of playing."

Bassist Milt Hinton in *OverTime* by Milt Hinton, David G. Berger and Holly Maxson, 1991

*Dizzy Gillespie, Chu Berry and Quentin Jackson, Fox Theater, Detroit, c. 1940. Photograph © Milton J. Hinton.*

*"King of 52nd St.," New York, c. 1948.*
*Photograph © 1979 William P. Gottlieb.*

"Cats would show up [at Minton's] who couldn't blow at all but would take six or seven choruses to prove it. So on afternoons before a session, Monk and I began to work out some complex variations on chords, and we'd use them at night to scare away the no-talent guys. After a while, we got interested in what we were doing as music, and as we began to explore more and more, our music evolved."

Dizzy in *Down Beat*, June 18, 1952

"Dizzy Gillespie is the quintessential bop trumpeter. He began developing his style, which grew out of Roy Eldridge's, while playing in Cab Calloway's orchestra in the early '40s. But Calloway was unimpressed. The Hi De Ho man responded to Gillespie's fiery, iconoclastic, humorous solos with an ultimatum: 'I don't want you playing that Chinese music on my band.'"

Critic Doug Ramsey in his book *Jazz Matters*, 1989

"I did a show with a disc jockey somewhere, and on a song called 'Simple Melody' I started doing a do-do-do-do-doodly-do, and this man said I was scat singing. I never considered it jazz or bop. I learned how to sing like that from Dizzy Gillespie."

Vocalist Ella Fitzgerald
in *Off the Record,*
by Joe Smith, 1988

*Ella Fitzgerald and Dizzy Gillespie, New York, 1948. Photograph © 1979 William P. Gottlieb.*

*The Royal Roost, New York, 1948. Photograph © Herman Leonard.*

*The Royal Roost, New York, 1948. Photograph © Herman Leonard.*

"First I play for myself, next I play for the musicians and then I hope the audience likes it. It's in that order. You might have to inspire a musician. One time a funny thing happened to me. I said to Teddy Stewart, the drummer, 'You're supposed to inspire the soloist.' He said, 'Have you ever thought that the soloist is supposed to inspire me?' I didn't say nothing else. It's true, we're all supposed to inspire each other to greater heights."

Dizzy in *Notes and Tones*, by Art Taylor, 1977

"Diz? I think he contributed 75 percent of modern music, as far as I'm concerned. That's right. I think he's one of the greatest."

Count Basie in
*to BE, or not . . . to BOP*,
by Dizzy Gillespie with Al Fraser,
1979

*Count Basie, Chicago, 1950. Photograph © Lee Tanner.*

"When I first heard Charlie Parker, I said, 'That's how our music should be played.' He had the phrasing, and he was a master blues player. I'd never heard anything like him. It was scary! After we got it together, yeah, I knew we were making something new. It was magic. Nobody on the planet was playing like that but us."

Dizzy in the *San Francisco Chronicle*, May 25, 1991

*Charlie Parker and Dizzy Gillespie, Birdland, New York, 1951. Photographer unknown, Frank Driggs Collection.*

"Dizzy Gillespie is an American paradox: a quintessentially critical and innovative artist who plays, often superbly, the clown. Of musicians of his stature, only Louis Armstrong and Fats Waller were his equal at walking the tightrope from jazz complexity to inspired silliness and back. Yet Armstrong and Waller played a relatively accessible music. Gillespie is a fearsome modernist—the man who, with Charlie Parker, invented jazz modernism in part to repudiate the very entertainment values that were thought to have dimmed the music's power during the commercially extravagant Swing Era."

Critic Gary Giddins in his article "Dizzy Like a Fox," *Grand Street*, 1991

*New York, 1953. Photograph © Herman Leonard.*

"'I love playing, I love people, I love making people laugh, and I do exactly what I want to do.' That's what Dizzy said to me recently, when I was amazed that at his age he was willing to start from scratch every evening, in a new club, a new town, in front of a new audience. . . . He's a monument to jazz . . . a pure soul."

Photographer Herman Leonard in his book *The Eye of Jazz,* 1985

*Dizzy Gillespie trumpet section (Quincy Jones at right), New York, 1953. Photograph © Herman Leonard.*

"He could teach anybody, but me. No man . . . the shit was going too fast."

Trumpeter Miles Davis
in *to BE or not . . . to BOP*,
by Dizzy Gillespie with Al Fraser,
1979

*Dizzy Gillespie and Miles Davis, Paris, 1958. Photograph © Herman Leonard.*

Teddy Wilson, Miles Davis, Dizzy Gillespie and Gerry Mulligan, Paris, 1958. Photograph © Herman Leonard.

"When I'm at Dizzy's house, the phone never stops ringing. Some musician is always asking Dizzy something, and he's never too busy. They have two lines for that purpose, just so Dizzy can discuss music. One day somebody called for the changes to a tune, and Dizzy went and pulled out his old charts and gave the correct changes over the phone. Diz has that love of musicians and that willingness to help out fellow musicians . . . more than anybody I see around now."

Pianist Hazel Scott in *Notes and Tones*, by Art Taylor, 1977

"The cooler or more intellectual forms mean reversion back to the original African. It's like modern painting and sculpture. The same thing with bop—Charlie Parker, Dizzy Gillespie and those people—that was in the direction of Africa."

Pianist/composer Duke Ellington
in *The World of Duke Ellington*,
by Stanley Dance, 1970

*Duke Ellington, Storeyville, Boston, 1958. Photograph © Lee Tanner.*

*New York, 1960. Photograph © 1991 William Claxton.*

"My cheeks started bulging out. I didn't get any physical pain from it, but all of a sudden, I looked like a frog whenever I played. I hadn't always played like that. . . . It was technically incorrect for playing with a symphony orchestra; but for what I wanted, it was perfectly correct."

Dizzy in his book *to BE, or not . . . to BOP*, 1979

47

Twenty-two Trumpet Players, Central Park, New York, 1961. Photograph © Herb Snitzer.

"I'm just in a long line of contributing trumpet players to the whole picture of jazz. I look at my stature as a major contributor to the music on the same scale as that of Buddy Bolden, King Oliver, Louis Armstrong, Roy Eldridge, Miles Davis and Clifford Brown. The message that a trumpet player brings is specific. All messengers have the same stature."

Dizzy in his book
*to BE, or not . . . to BOP*, 1979

1. Buck Clayton  2. Roy Eldridge  3. Dizzy Gillespie  4. Charlie Shavers  5. Herman Autrey
6. Joe Newman  7. Dizzy Reece  8. Freddie Hubbard  9. Red Allen  10. Don Ferrara  11. Nick Travis
12. Bobby Bradford  13. Joe Thomas  14. Yank Lawson  15. Clark Terry  16. Jimmy Nottingham
17. Ernie Royal  18. Johnny Letman  19. Booker Little  20. Doc Severinsen  21. Max Kaminsky
22. Ted Curson

*New York, 1962. Photograph © Charles Stewart.*

"I don't make a habit of wishing for what I don't have, but I often wish I had a lighter nature. Dizzy has that beautiful gift. I can't say, 'Be happy, people.' It's something I can't command. But you have to be true to your own nature."

Saxophonist John Coltrane in *Jazz Anecdotes*, by Bill Crow, 1990

*John Coltrane, The Jazz Workshop, Boston, 1963. Photograph © Lee Tanner.*

*Newport Jazz Festival, Newport, Rhode Island, 1963. Photograph © Lee Tanner.*

"When he takes to his horn, Gillespie's cheeks puff out like a squirrel busy getting set for a hard winter. His neck swells, the nether tuft bristles, his eyes screw up behind the heavy, black-rimmed glasses, and a strange assembly of notes skitters forth."

Critic J. P. Cahn in the *San Francisco Chronicle,* October 3, 1948

"At seven I was listening to Gene Austin and singing the pop songs of the day. When I was fourteen and working with Art Tatum, Louis Armstrong was my idol. Returning from Europe at the end of World War II I heard 'Salt Peanuts' and then all I wanted to do was play and sing bebop . . . and when it came to singing, I followed Dizzy."

Vocalist Jon Hendricks

Jon Hendricks and Dizzy Gillespie, Monterey Jazz Festival, Monterey, California, 1963. Photograph © Jerry Stoll.

"His innovations have penetrated not merely throughout the five continents but through all the idioms of jazz that followed his arrival. A Gillespie phrase, a melodic twist or turn that swirled out of the tilted bell of his horn decades ago, may be found today in the most improbable of places, from pop to rock."

Critic Leonard Feather, *Los Angeles Times*, 1977

*New York, 1965. Photograph © Charles Stewart.*

"John Birks is a human being I admire greatly. . . . He was never too busy to listen and help with questions of life and living when he could. Never sentimental, always supportive . . . he was the father I lost when I was eleven."

Bassist Chris White

*Chris White, Dizzy Gillespie and James Moody, Monterey Jazz Festival, Monterey, California, 1965. Photograph © Jerry Stoll.*

"I was in junior high school with Eric Dolphy, and one day he asked me to come to his house to hear some new stuff. Then I heard Dizzy Gillespie, and that did it. I said, 'This is what I want to play!' It was the hippest music I had ever heard in my life."

Pianist Hampton Hawes in *Notes and Tones*, by Art Taylor, 1977

*Hampton Hawes, WGBH-TV, Boston, 1966. Photograph © Lee Tanner.*

"I didn't want to be a bandleader until after I played with him, and aside from being the best on his instrument, I used to admire the way he had control of the audience, or how he would get control of the audience and hold it. He's got it all together."

Pianist Junior Mance in *to Be, or not . . . . to BOP,* by Dizzy Gillespie with Al Fraser, 1979

*Junior Mance, WGBH-TV, Boston, 1967. Photograph © Lee Tanner.*

"Dizzy Gillespie had a lot to do with the popularity of the conga. He included Chano Pozo in his band and started to develop things like 'Manteca,' 'Tin Tin Deo' and the others. You can't say how great the Gillespie/Pozo relationship was. The importance is blurred a little. You accept the conga now, but it was only bongos and timbales at one time."

Conga drummer
Mongo Santamaria in
*Down Beat,* April 21, 1977

Mongo Santamaria, WGBH-TV, Boston, 1968. Photograph © Lee Tanner.

*Bergamo, Italy, 1968. Photograph © Giuseppe Pino.*

*Thelonious Monk, WGBH-TV, Boston, 1968. Photograph © Lee Tanner.*

"I go for freedom, but freedom without organization is chaos. I want to put freedom into music the way I conceive it. It is free, but it's organized freedom. You've got to take memory from the universe. Man will never organize anything as well as nature can. It's perpetual, but so many things are happening that you can always discover something else in nature."

Dizzy in *Notes and Tones*, by Art Taylor, 1977

"Every sound influenced Diz. He had that kind of mind, you know? And he influenced everything too."

Thelonious Monk in
*Down Beat*, April 21, 1966

"I decided I liked the horn bent because I can hear a note the minute I hit it. This way I can hear my mistakes faster."

Dizzy in *American Way,*
September 15, 1990

*Milan, Italy, 1971. Photograph © Giuseppe Pino.*

"He's not just clowning up there. He's playing beautiful, beautiful stuff!"

Bassist Charles Mingus

*Dizzy Gillespie and Charles Mingus, Newport Jazz Festival, Newport, Rhode Island, 1971. Photograph © Milton J. Hinton.*

*Carmen McRae and Dizzy Gillespie, Great American Music Hall, San Francisco, 1976. Photograph © 1992 Jim Marshall.*

"Dizzy differed from the majority of bebop pioneer-outlaws in his refusal to seek refuge in self-pity, self-destruction and their handmaiden, drug abuse, which wasted so many of his compatriots. Thanks to vast reserves of mental health, a secure sense of his own value, a remarkable lack of envy and an irrepressible humor and gusto for living, Dizzy survives today as an elder statesman, still creating, refusing to coast on past contributions that are as manifold as they are little understood."

Critic Grover Sales in his book *Jazz, America's Classical Music*, 1984

"I recently said to Dizzy, 'You never had any children of your own. . . . Well, we're all your children musically and spiritually.'"

Trumpeter Jimmy Owens

*Jimmy Owens, Newark, New Jersey, 1977. Photograph © Lee Tanner.*

*Montreaux Jazz Festival, Switzerland, 1977. Photograph © Giuseppe Pino.*

62

*Great American Music Hall, San Francisco, 1978. Photograph © 1992 Bruce Polonsky.*

"As a musician, I think Dizzy has no peer. He's inspired perhaps more musicians who are out here today than you can shake a stick at. And I mean not just trumpet players or saxophone players but percussion people as well. Dizzy was always a complete musician, both as a composer, orchestrator and, of course, one of the most innovative of soloists on trumpet."

Drummer Max Roach

*Dizzy Gillespie and Roy Haynes, Great American Music Hall, San Francisco, 1979. Photograph © 1992 Bruce Polonsky.*

"In improvisation, the first thing you must have is the sight of a gifted painter. You've got to see colors and lines in music, and then you've got to be able to mix the colors and draw the lines. The better you mix colors and draw lines, the better the painting is going to be."

Dizzy in his book *to BE, or not . . . to BOP,* 1979

"I've always been a Latin freak. Very early in my career, I realized that our music and that of our brothers in Latin America had a common source. The Latin musician was fortunate in one sense. They didn't take the drum away from him, so he was more polyrhythmic."

Dizzy in his book *to BE, or not . . . to BOP,* 1979

*Great American Music Hall, San Francisco, 1979. Photograph © 1992 Bruce Polonsky.*

"Dizzy is truly simple as he wants to be, but he's sly as a fox and smart as a whip. Now that's why we call him Dizzy."

Vocalist Sarah Vaughan

*Nice, France, 1981. Photograph © Milton J. Hinton.*

*Montreaux Jazz Festival, Switzerland, 1980. Photograph © Andy Freeberg.*

"Jazz is the one thing that we have that the whole world wants. It's a kind of meeting place where one man can feel what another does even if they speak different languages. There's a kind of directness—with no middle man—between the artist and his public."

Dizzy in the *San Francisco Chronicle*, January 27, 1957

*Dizzy Gillespie and John Faddis, New York, 1982. Photographs © Carol Friedman.*

*Dizzy Gillespie and John Faddis, New York, 1982. Photograph © Carol Friedman.*

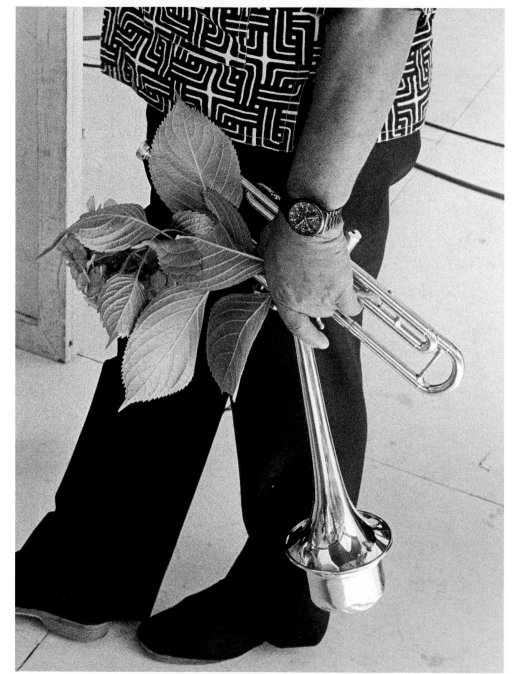

"The first thing we must keep in mind about a musician is that the music he plays is a reflection of his true self. His music might not be what you, the listener, thinks he is, but truly, he can no more escape himself through his playing than we can escape the contingent world in which we are placed, except through death. You are what you are; that is reality, you can't escape it. And the reality of the musician—especially the jazz musician—is that the music is a continuance of himself."

Dizzy in *Jazz People*, by Ole Brask, 1976

*Charleston, South Carolina, 1984. Photograph © W. Patrick Hinely.*

*"Wolf Trap Salutes John Birks 'Dizzy' Gillespie,"* with, left to right, Jon Faddis, Freddie Hubbard, Jimmy Owens and Wynton Marsalis, Wolf Trap, Virginia, 1987. Photograph © Michael Wilderman.

"Dizzy Gillespie is the most beautiful cat that I've ever met. Here's a cat that convinced me that everything is hip. He'll talk you to death, and he knows. He's beautiful. He's a serious, funny cat."

Freddie Hubbard in *Notes and Tones,* by Art Taylor, 1977

"'Be-Bop' is the name of a song written by Dizzy Gillespie. As far as I can remember, critics called the music bebop when they came into the club where we were playing at that particular time on 52nd Street. The music was so unique and unusual, so fresh and original; they asked Dizzy what he called it, and perhaps Dizzy misunderstood their question, or maybe he told them the title of the tune. At that particular time, I remember, we were playing a song called 'Be-Bop,' and they just called all the music bebop. It's another one of those nicknames like boy, nigger and jazz."

Drummer Max Roach in
*Notes and Tones*, by Art Taylor,
1977

*Max Roach, Oakland, California, 1987. Photograph © Lee Tanner.*

"It was new, and it was fresh, and here's a guy who was creating a crazy sump'n entirely new, but it was so inventive. The harmonies, the chord structure, and the skill with which it was being played. He had a part where he jumped a couple of octaves, 'Baa-Bee!' Like that. And it was really outstanding playing."

Lionel Hampton in
*to BE, or not . . . to BOP,*
by Dizzy Gillespie with Al Fraser,
1979

*Lionel Hampton and Dizzy Gillespie, Montreaux Jazz Festival, Switzerland, 1988. Photograph © Herb Snitzer.*

"Dizzy has always had a certain joie de vivre combined with a childlike innocence and curiosity about life. Just watching Dizzy with children is a joy, especially after he appeared on "The Muppet Show" with Kermit the Frog. Dizzy would put his finger to his lips, puff his cheeks, and the kids would just start giggling—instant Dizzy fans."

Trumpeter Jon Faddis

*With the Muppets, London, 1988. Photograph © Herman Leonard, courtesy Henson Associates, Inc.*

74

James Moody and Bill Bell, San Francisco, 1990. Photograph © Lee Tanner.

"Every time I get on the bandstand with him is a musical lesson. Sometimes little bits of wisdom he imparts will come back to me years later and I'll say, 'Ah!'"

Saxophonist James Moody
in *American Way*,
September 15, 1991

"Dizzy worked on chord progressions . . . finding different ways of doing things. Finding different progressions, alternate ways of using the musical chords, not just the given things that are in the songs. He would work out the alternates and prettier themes, different progressions to them, and countermelodies, which he still does. Man, there are some beautiful passages that Dizzy has created."

Vocalist Billy Eckstine in *to BE, or not . . . to BOP*, by Dizzy Gillespie with Al Fraser, 1979

*Dizzy Gillespie and Billy Eckstine, Montgomery College, Rockville, Maryland, 1989. Photograph © Michael Wilderman.*

*With the United Nations Orchestra, North Sea Jazz Festival, The Hague, The Netherlands, 1990. Photograph © Tad Hershorn.*

"The basic thing about jazz music is putting the notes to rhythm, not the other way around. . . . I think up a rhythm first and then I put notes to it to correspond with the chord. You can play very, very beautiful notes, and if it doesn't have any rhythmic form, it doesn't amount to anything."

Dizzy in the *San Francisco Chronicle*, May 3, 1959.

"It's taken me all my life to learn what not to play."

Dizzy in *Jazz Is*, by Nat Hentoff, 1976

*Emeryville, California, 1992. Photograph © Jeff Sedlik.*

*Emeryville, California, 1992. Photograph © Jeff Sedlik.*

"Musically, the most important facet of Dizzy's playing is not just his rhythm, harmony, chord changes or his technical facility alone. It's the whole thing. Knowing that horn, he can do anything with it."

Cab Calloway in
*to BE, or not . . . to BOP,*
by Dizzy Gillespie with Al Fraser,
1979

*Dizzy Gillespie, Panama Francis and Cab Calloway, recording studio, New Jersey, 1990. Photograph © 1991 Milton J. Hinton.*

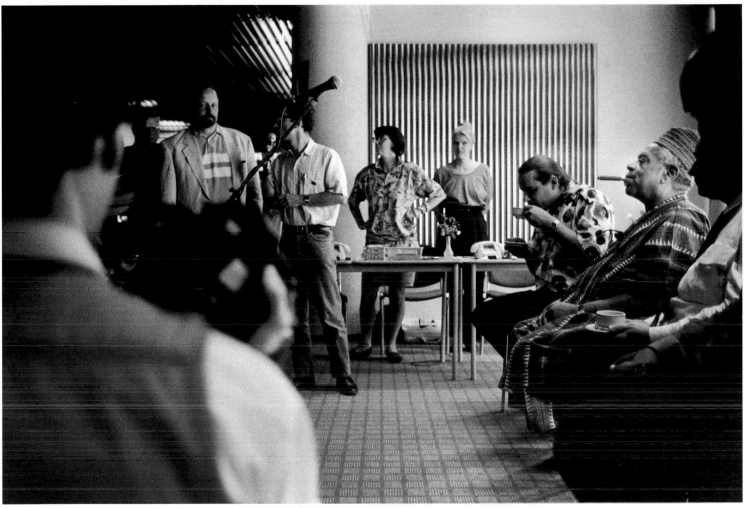

*Press conference, North Sea Jazz Festival, The Hague, The Netherlands, 1990. Photograph © W. Patrick Hinely.*

"Now Diz is dizzy like a fox, you know. He's one of the smartest guys around. Musically, he knows what he is doing backwards and forwards. So what he hears . . . goes in and stays. Later, he'll go home and figure it all out just what it is. So the arranging, the chord progressions and things in progressive music, Dizzy is responsible for. You have to say that."

Vocalist Billy Eckstine in
*Talking Jazz*, by Max Jones, 1987

"Dizzy's funny when he sings. He makes me laugh, but I love it. I love when he sings, and Dizzy's a good arranger, he's a great arranger. Dizzy's what a good musician is supposed to be."

Vocalist Sarah Vaughan

Houston, Texas, 1990. Photograph © Tad Hershorn.

*Los Angeles, 1990. Photograph © Marlene Wallace.*

*Miriam Makeba and Dizzy Gillespie, Europe, 1991. Photograph © Dany Gignoux.*

"A student of music, if he goes back far enough, will find out that the main source of our music is Africa. The music of the Western Hemisphere (not just our music)—the music of Cuba, the music of Brazil, the music of the West Indies, although they haven't made such a big impact on humanity as a whole, as jazz, spirituals and blues which were created by the blacks in the United States—is primarily of African origin."

Dizzy Gillespie in his book
*to BE, or not . . . to BOP,* 1979

"He always wanted to change my way of walking chords, which was straight-down-the-middle. Since I knew the tune I'd be soloing on in the next show, he'd take it apart harmonically and give me flatted chords and very modern substitutions to use. Whenever I had trouble understanding, he'd demonstrate by playing the bass line, on his horn, note for note. By the end of the break I usually had an idea of how I'd play my next solo."

Bassist Milt Hinton in *Bass Line* by Milt Hinton and David G. Berger, 1988

*Milt Hinton, Kimball's East, Emeryville, California, 1991. Photograph © Lee Tanner.*

"There is a parallel with jazz and religion. In jazz a messenger comes to the music and spreads his influences to a certain point, and then another comes and takes you further. In religion—in the spiritual sense—God picks certain individuals from this world to lead mankind up to a certain point of spiritual development."

Dizzy in his book
*to BE. or not . . . to BOP.* 1979

*Oakland, California, 1988. Photograph © 1992 Michael Collopy.*

"His thoughts, his musical concepts and his feelings make him a major musician, period. If I have to make comparisons with art in other forms: Picasso in painting. He has a sense of humor and the use of the line like Picasso does."

Pianist Lalo Schifrin in
*to BE, or not . . . to BOP,*
by Dizzy Gillespie
with Al Fraser, 1979

*Emeryville, California, 1992. Photograph © Jeff Sedlik.*